Salvington Mill

FA
SU
RECIPES

compiled by
Pat Smith

with illustrations
by A.R. Quinton

SALMON

Index

Apple and Cranberry Pie 37
Apple Cracknell 43
Artichoke Pie 11
Blackberry Water Ice 31
Brighton Gingerbread 29
Cherry Tart from Ripe 34
Elderberry Chutney 15
Fitzherbert Pudding 35
Goodwood Herrings 38
Lady Monmouth's Cheese Cake 32
Lady Pettus's Biscakes 7
Lobster or Crab Pie 30
Military Pudding 27
Pippin Pie 5
Plum Heavies 23
Rabbit Stew 46
Rother Rabbit 6

Selsey Herring 14
Shepherd's Wheel Pie 24
Shrimp Toast 22
Sloe and Apple Jelly 10
Sloe Gin 18
Sorrel and Leek Pie 16
Susannah Hooker's 1828 Punch 26
Sussex Cream 21
Sussex Pond Pudding 8
Sussex Potato and Cheese Cakes 13
Sussex Pudding 45
Sussex Rolls 40
Sussex Sausage Rolls 3
Ten-to-One Pie 42
Walnut Cakes 39
Windmill Hill Thin Biscuits 47
Winkinhurst Girdle Cakes 19

Cover pictures: *front* The South Downs and Chanctonbury Ring; *back* Felpham

Printed and Published by J. Salmon Ltd., Sevenoaks, England ©

Sussex Sausage Rolls or Hikers' Lunch

1¼ lb. bread dough
1 lb. sausages or sausagemeat

Cut off pieces of dough and wrap them around each skinned sausage or the equivalent sausagemeat. The dough should be ¼ inch–½ inch thick. Leave to rise in a greased tin in a warm place for 20 minutes or until well risen. Bake at 425°F of Mark 7 for 15 minutes and then reduce the temperature to 350 °F or Mark 4 for a further 20 minutes.

This is a very old recipe. It is recommended that they are eaten in the open air anywhere in Sussex, preferably on the Downs!

The River Cuckmere at Alfriston

Pippin Pie

2 eating apples per person preferably pippins
1 orange to every 4 apples
1 piece of cinnamon stick per apple
1 or 2 cloves per apple
Almonds
Sultanas
8 oz. shortcrust pastry

Set oven to 375°F or Mark 5. Peel and core the apples. Place in a greased pie dish. Fill each centre with a few almonds, sultanas and a piece of cinnamon stick. Push cloves into each apple and sprinkle with the grated rind from the oranges. Pour the orange juice over the apples. Cover the dish with pastry and cook for approximately 35–40 minutes until the apples are cooked and the pastry is brown.

Rother Rabbit

1 rabbit (jointed)
Wine glass of wine vinegar
1 oz. butter
1 large onion
½ lb. prunes
Elderberry wine
Flour
English mustard powder
1 teaspoon allspice
½ teaspoon mace
1 tablespoon chopped marjoram or
2 teaspoons dried marjoram
Salt and Pepper

Soak the rabbit overnight in salt water to which the vinegar has been added. Set oven to 400°F or Mark 6. Soften the onion in butter, drain and place in a greased casserole with the prunes. Drain and dry the joints and toss them in the flour, mixed with some mustard powder. Brown the joints in the butter and put into the casserole. Add the spices and herbs and cover the meat with the wine. Season. Place casserole in oven and when it boils, approximately 15 minutes, reduce temperature to 325°F or Mark 3 for a further 1¾ hours, or until tender. Adjust seasoning. Serve with broccoli. Serves 4.

Lady Pettus's Biscakes

8 oz. self-raising flour
6 oz. caster sugar
4 oz. butter
3 oz. hazlenuts, roasted and ground
3 eggs, separated
Grated peel of a large lemon
4 teaspoons orange 'flower water'

ICING
2 tablespoons apricot jam
6 oz. icing sugar
Juice of 1 lemon
28 hazelnuts, roasted
28 small paper baking cases

Set oven to 400°F or Mark 6. Whip the egg whites until stiff. Cream the butter, sugar and lemon peel. Beat in the egg yolk. Fold in the egg whites, flour, orange flower water and ground nuts. If the mixture is stiff add a little milk. Put a heaped teaspoonful into each paper case and bake for about 10–15 minutes until firm and golden. Meanwhile warm the jam in a saucepan; mix in the icing sugar and enough lemon juice to make a stiff consistency. Place a teaspoonful of this mixture on each cake, topping with a nut as soon as removed from the oven. Return to the oven for 2 minutes.

Sussex Pond Pudding

PASTRY
8 oz. self-raising flour
4 oz. suet
2 oz. fresh white breadcrumbs
Pinch of salt
Milk and water to mix

FILLING
1 lemon
4 oz. brown sugar
4 oz. butter

Mix the dry ingredients for the pastry, using the milk and water to form them into a soft dough. Reserve one third of the dough for the lid. Roll out the remainder into a circle and line a greased 2 pint pudding basin. Leave some pastry overlapping the edge. Prick the lemon all over with clean knitting needle, smear with the butter and roll in the sugar. Place in the lined basin together with any remaining sugar and butter. Roll out the remaining pastry into a circle. Use this to make a lid, sealing it with a little water. Cover with greased paper and a cloth or foil. Steam for 3–4 hours. Serves 6.

Mermaid Street, Rye

Sloe and Apple Jelly

Equal quantities of sloes and apples
Water
Granulated sugar

Rinse the fruit and cut the apples into pieces; do not peel. Put all the fruit into a pan, cover with cold water and bring to the boil. Cook until soft. Put into a jelly bag and allow to drip. When strained, measure the juice and allow 1 lb. sugar to every pint. Heat together, gently, until *ALL* the sugar is dissolved. Then bring to the boil and boil rapidly until setting point is reached. Put into warm pots and cover.

Artichoke Pie

2 lb. Jerusalem artichokes
2 lb. cooked mashed potatoes
1 oz. butter
1 tablespoon plain flour
Salt
1 tablespoon grated cheese

Set oven to 400°F or Mark 6. Clean and peel the artichokes. Boil in salt water until tender. Drain and keep the water. Melt the butter and stir in the flour, and use approximately ½ pint of the artichoke water to make a fairly thick sauce. Line a greased pie dish with mashed potatoes. Fill the centre with the cooked artichokes and cover with the sauce. Season and sprinkle with grated cheese. Bake in a hot oven for approximately 25–30 minutes until brown.

A mixture of roots can be used if preferred.

Eleven

Arundel from the River Arun

Sussex Potato and Cheese Cakes

8 oz. cooked, mashed potatoes
½ oz. butter
2 shallots, chopped
2oz. flour
2 oz. grated cheese
1 beaten egg

First soften the shallots in the butter. Then mix all the ingredients together and form into small round cakes. Cook on a pre-heated griddle or a heavy frying pan. Can also be cooked on a baking sheet in a hot oven, 400°F or Mark 6 for 10–15 minutes. Serve with poached or fried eggs and/or grilled bacon rashers.

Selsey Herrings

6 herrings, cleaned and filleted
1 tablespoon malt or wine vinegar

SAUCE
4 tablespoons single cream
3 tablespoons grated horseradish
2 tablespoons white vinegar
½ teaspoon salt
1 teaspoon tarragon vinegar
Pinch of cayenne pepper
Pinch of dry mustard
Pinch of caster sugar

'Ready-made' horseradish sauce could be substituted for the fresh horseradish

Set oven to 375°F or Mark 5. Roll up each fillet, including roes, and secure with a skewer or cotton. Put into a greased ovenproof dish. Pour a little vinegar over each roll. Add cold water until the rolls are half submerged. Bake for about ½ hour. Meanwhile grate the horesradish and add to the rest of the ingredients; blend thoroughly. Leave the fillets to get cold. Serve with a green salad and the sauce. Serves 6.

Fourteen

Elderberry Chutney

1 lb. elderberries
1 lb. cooking apples
1 lb. onions
8 oz. seedless raisins
1½ pints malt or wine vinegar
3 oz. root ginger
1 tablespoon mustard seed
1 teaspoon pickling spice
1 teaspoon salt
2 lb. sugar

Wash the elderberries and place in a pan with some of the vinegar. Cook until soft, pass through a sieve, discard the pips etc. and then return the pulp to the pan. Add the peeled and cored apples, raisins and the rest of the vinegar. Bruise the ginger and place in a piece of muslin together with the mustard seed and spice, fold up and tie and add to the pan. Cook until all is tender, then add the salt and sugar and stir until the sugar is dissolved. Cook slowly until the mixture thickens. Pot into warm jars and cover.

Sorrel and Leek Pie

8 oz. shortcrust pastry
6 oz. sorrel or spinach
6 oz. leeks
6 rashers of bacon

Salty bacon should be put into cold water and brought to the boil to reduce the salt, then drain before using.

Set oven at 400°F or Mark 6. Line a 6½ inch–7 inch plate or flan tin with shortcrust pastry. Put in a layer or sorrel or spinach (plenty as it will shrink), a layer of bacon, then some sliced leeks, more bacon and finally a layer of sorrel. Season; beware of too much salt if the bacon is salty. Cover with a pastry lid and bake for 1½ hours.

East Beach, Hastings

Sloe Gin

Sloes
Gin
Granulated sugar

Prick each sloe with a darning needle. Half fill clean, dry wine or spirit bottles with the fruit and add approximately 3 oz. sugar to each 1 lb. sloes. Cover with gin, cork firmly and shake well. Keep in a warm place and shake each day for several weeks. After 3 months, strain the liqueur through muslin into clean bottles, cork well and leave to mature. More sugar can be added later if too sour. Improves with keeping.

Winkinhurst Girdle Cake

3 oz. butter
1 tablespoon brown sugar
4 oz. currants
6 oz. self-raising flour
Milk to mix
Pinch of salt

Melt the butter and add the sugar and the currants. Remove from heat, add the flour and bind the mixture with the milk. Roll out to ¼ inch thickness in a circle. Cut into 4 quarters and cook on a greased pre-heated griddle or heavy frying pan. Cook on each side for about 15–20 minutes in all. Wrap in a clean cloth and serve warm with butter.

The Gateway, Battle Abbey

Sussex Cream

1 pint milk
4 egg yolks
4 oz. sugar
4 oz. macaroons or ratafia biscuits
2 x ½ oz. packets gelatine
3 oz. glacé cherries, chopped
Rind and juice of 1 orange
½ glass sherry
½ pint double cream

DECORATION
2 glacé cherries, quartered
8 segments fresh orange

Pour 3 tablespoons milk into a small bowl and stand in some hot water. Sprinkle the gelatine on to the milk and leave to melt. Whisk the yolks with a little of the remaining milk. Bring the rest of the milk to the boil with the rind of the orange. Add the macaroons and the sugar to the hot milk and whisk in the yolk mixture. Stir continuously until the mixture thickens. Add the gelatine mixture, orange juice and sherry. Strain the mixture and leave to cool. When nearly set, whip the cream until thick but not stiff and whisk well into the cooled mixture. Fold in the cherries. Pour into a wetted mould or dish. When set, turn out and decorate with cherries. Pour into a wetted mould or dish. When set, turn out and decorate with cherries and orange segments. Serves 8.

Shrimp Toast

2 egg yolks
1 teaspoon anchovy essence
1 tablespoon milk
½ pint peeled shrimps

Mix the egg yolks with the anchovy essence, the milk and the shrimps. Warm the mixture gently in a saucepan, stirring continuously until the sauce thickens slightly. Remove from the heat and serve on hot buttered toast. Serve 2.

Plum Heavies

1 lb. flour
4 oz. butter
2 oz. lard
4 oz. sugar
4 oz. currants
Milk

Set oven to 375°F or Mark 5. Rub the fats into the flour and add the sugar and fruit. Mix into a soft dough with milk. Roll out to about ½ inch thickness and cut into rounds with a small pastry cutter. Bake for about 10–15 minutes until light brown.

Mothers sometimes made Heavies from leftover pastry into which dried fruit was pressed. They were then given to the children as snacks, so they were always small.

Shepherd's Wheel Pie

1 lb. minced or thinly sliced cooked lamb
1 medium onion
2 oz. mushrooms, chopped
2 sticks celery, chopped
½ clove garlic, chopped
½ oz. butter
2 heaped tablespoons elderberry or fruit chutney
Stock to moisten
Seasoning
1 lb. cooked mashed potatoes
1 carrot sliced lengthwise and blanched

Set oven to 350°F or Mark 4. Place meat into a 6 inch–7 inch greased round pie dish. Soften the onion, celery, mushrooms and garlic in a little butter. Add them to the meat, with the chutney and some stock. Mix thoroughly. Cover with the potato. Make grooves radiating from the centre like spokes of a wheel and lay the carrot slices in them. Dot with butter. Cook until the meat is bubbling well and the potato is brown; about 20 minutes. Serves 4.

Chanctonbury Ring, South Downs

Susannah Hooker's 1828 Punch

SHERBERT
2 large fresh lemons
Lumps of sugar
Boiling water

FOR 8 PINTS PUNCH
4 pints sherbert
1 pint rum
1 pint brandy
2 pints ale

Rub the sugar lumps over the lemons until they have absorbed all the zest and place in a large bowl. Squeeze the lemons and add the pulp and most of the juice to the sugar lumps. Mash together thoroughly. Taste. If the mixture is not too acidic add the remaining juice and mix with boiling water to make approximately 4 pints. Cool and strain. This is called Sherbert. Mix the brandy and rum in equal quantities and add to the sherbert. Ale can be used instead of brandy or can be added as well to give extra richness.

This recipe is very much to personal taste and purse!

Military Pudding

6 oz. breadcrumbs
3 oz. suet
1 tablespoon ground rice
Grated rind and juice of a lemon
1 large or 2 small eggs
Stoned raisins

Mix together all the ingredients, except the raisins, to make a fairly wet mixture. If too dry add a little milk. Grease a 1 pint pudding basin and scatter raisins over the base. Pour the mixture on top. Cover with greased paper and a cloth or foil. Steam for 2½ hours.

The Beach, Brighton

Brighton Gingerbread - *a light gingerbread*

6 oz. butter
6 oz. caster sugar
3 eggs
3 oz. black treacle
8 oz. flour
1 teaspoon mixed spice
1 teaspoon ground ginger
Scant ½ teaspoon baking powder
2–4 oz. flaked almonds
3 tablespoons milk

Set oven to 350°F or Mark 4. Cream the butter and sugar and add the eggs, beating them in well. Sift all the dry ingredients together and fold into the creamed mixture with the treacle. Fold in the almonds and milk. Pour into a lined tin approximately 8 inch square. Bake for approximately ¾ hour until firm.

Lobster or Crab Pie

The meat from 2 medium-size fresh lobsters, approximately ½ lb. each (reserve contents of the heads and the coral) or 3 medium-size fresh crabs (reserve brown meat and treat same as lobster 'head and coral' meat)
8 oz. shortcrust pastry
¼–½ pint single cream
2 hardboiled eggs
Lemon juice
Seasoning
Ground mace
Butter

Set oven to 400°F or Mark 6. Line a 6½ inch–7 inch greased baking tin with pastry. Place a layer of the meat on to the pastry. Season with salt, pepper and mace. Add a little lemon juice and dot with butter. Add a layer of sliced egg. Repeat layers with the remaining meat and eggs. Cover with a pastry lid. Cook for 40–45 minutes until the filling is sizzling. Meanwhile mix the head and coral meat with enough cream to make a sauce. When baked lift the lid and pour the sauce over the contents. Replace lid. Serve with a green salad. A layer of oysters can be added, before baking, if desired.

Blackberry Water Ice

1½ lb. blackberries, giving approximately ½ pint juice
6 oz. granulated sugar
1½ gills water

Dissolve the sugar in the water, then bring to the boil and continue boiling in an open pan for 20 minutes. Meanwhile press the berries through a nylon sieve. When the syrup is cool, stir it into the puree. Do not make it too sweet (any remaining syrup will keep in a screw-top jar in the refrigerator; use to sweeten other fruit dishes). Freeze, whisking several times before it is frozen, approximately 2½–3 hours. Serves 4.

Lady Monmouth's Cheese Cake

PASTRY
8 oz. plain flour
4 oz. butter
1 oz. caster sugar
1 egg yolk
1 teaspoon rosewater

FILLING
¼ pint double cream
8 oz. curd or cream cheese
2 oz. caster sugar
2 eggs, separated
2 teaspoons orange flower water
2 oz. flaked almonds
4 oz. currants or chopped glacé ginger
Mixed nuts

Set oven to 400°F or Mark 6. Rub the butter into the flour. Mix the yolk, sugar and rosewater together and add to the dry ingredients to make a paste (a little water may be needed). Roll out and line a fairly deep 9 inch flan tin. For the filling whip the cream until fairly thick and add the cheese beaten with the sugar. Add the orange water to the egg yolks and blend with the cream mixture. Beat the whites until stiff and fold into the mixture together with the currants and ginger and the almonds. Fill the pastry case and sprinkle with the mixed nuts. Bake for 10 minutes; reduce oven temperature to 325°F or Mark 3 and continue baking until filling is set, approximately 1 hour. The mixture will rise during cooking. Serves 8.

Crowborough Beacon from Frant

Cherry Tart from Ripe

PASTRY
8 oz. plain flour
Pinch of salt
1 oz. cornflour
2 level teaspoons icing sugar
4 oz. lard and margarine mixed
1 egg yolk
2 tablespoons cold water

FILLING
1 lb. black cherries, stoned
(if using canned cherries, drain well)
4 oz. icing sugar
2 eggs
3 oz. ground almonds
Almond essence

Set oven to 400°F or Mark 6. Sift the flour, salt, cornflour and icing sugar into a bowl. Rub in the mixed fat and bind to a dough with the egg yolk and water. Knead the pastry lightly and roll out. Line a 9 inch fluted flan ring on a greased baking sheet. Bake blind for 15 minutes. Reduce oven temperature to 325°F or Mark 3. Arrange cherries in the pastry case. Mix the sugar, eggs and almonds together with a little essence and pour the mixture over the cherries. Bake for 50–60 minutes until firm and golden. Serve hot or cold with cream.

Fitzherbert Pudding

1 lb. cooking apple pulp
3 oz. sugar
3 eggs, well beaten
3 oz. fresh breadcrumbs
3 teaspoons orange flower water
A little grated nutmeg
Grated rind of a lemon
A few flaked almonds
1 tablespoon demerara sugar
10 oz. puff or flaky pastry

Set oven to 425°F or Mark 7. Heat the apple pulp in a saucepan and then dissolve the sugar in it. Cool slightly and add the eggs, nutmeg, lemon rind, orange flower water and breadcrumbs. Line a 9 inch flan tin with thinly rolled pastry. Threequarters fill the flan with the pulp mixture; it will rise in the cooking. Scatter the almonds and demerara sugar over the top and bake until the filling is set and the pastry brown, approximately 20–30 minutes. Serves 8.

Beachy Head, Eastbourne

Apple and Cranberry Pie

1¼ cooking apples
2 oz. sugar
3 oz. cranberries
Lemon juice
Lemon rind
4 cloves
Grated nutmeg
6 oz. shortcrust pastry

Set oven to 375°F or Mark 5. Peel and slice the apples and keep in salted water to prevent browning. Boil the cores and the peel with the sugar for ½ hour. Strain and use the juice to sweeten the layers of fruit. Put a layer of apples in a pie dish, then a layer of cranberries, not too many, just enough to give a tang to the flavour. Sprinkle with a little lemon juice, lemon rind and grated nutmeg. Add some of the apple syrup and the cloves. Repeat until the pie dish is full. Cover with shortcrust pastry. Bake for 25–30 minutes or until the fruit is tender. Serves 4–5.

Goodwood Herrings

6 herrings
6 large tomatoes
4 tablespoons breadcrumbs
1 tablespoon chopped parsley
A little lemon rind
A small onion, finely chopped
A little thyme or fresh dill
1 tablespoon butter
Salt and pepper

Set oven to 375°F or Mark 5. Clean, scale and behead the herrings but leave the tails on and the roes inside. Curl each fish head to tail and fasten with a skewer. Slice the top off each tomato and reserve. Scoop out the pulp, discarding the core and mix with the breadcrumbs, herbs, onion, lemon rind, pepper and salt. Fill each tomato with this mixture, place a little butter on each one and replace the tops, Place a tomato in the centre of each curled fish. Place in a greased ovenproof dish and bake for 20 minutes.

Walnut Cakes

4 oz. walnuts
1 egg white
1 tablespoon self-raising flour
4 oz. caster sugar
1 teaspoon orange flower water
Extra walnuts

Set oven to 375°F or Mark 5. Pound the nuts in a mortar or electric grinder until well ground. Beat the egg white until stiff. Add the sugar and beat until thick. Beat in the flour, walnuts and orange water until well mixed. Put separate teaspoonfuls of the mixture on to a greased baking tray and place a walnut in the centre of each. Bake for approximately 10–15 minutes until pale brown.

Sussex Rolls

1¼ lb. bread dough
6 oz. butter and 3 oz. lard (mixed together)
2 oz. of the fat can be replaced by 2 oz. of cheese; this can be put on the paste in a fourth rolling

Set oven to 425°F or Mark 7. Put the fat in a cool place, it should be firm but not hard. Roll out the dough to approximately 6 inch x 18 inch. Coarsely spread ⅓ of the fat on ⅔ of the length of dough. Fold the empty part on to the middle ⅓ and fold the top ⅓ down over the other two (the same method as flaky pastry). Repeat twice. Finally roll out to ½ inch thickness. Cut with a knife (dipped in hot water) into squares or diamonds and put on to a greased baking sheet. Prove for 35–40 minutes, until well risen. Bake for 20 minutes. Makes approximately 15 rolls.

METRIC CONVERSIONS

The weights, measures and oven temperatures used in the preceding recipes can be easily converted to their metric equivalents.

Weights

Avoirdupois	Metric
1 oz.	just under 30 grams
4 oz. (¼ lb.)	app. 115 grams
8 oz. (½ lb.)	app. 230 grams
1 lb.	454 grams

Liquid Measures

Imperial	Metric
1 tablespoon (liquid only)	20 millilitres
1 fl. oz.	app. 30 millilitres
1 gill (¼ pt.)	app. 145 millilitres
½ pt.	app. 285 millilitres
1 pt.	app. 570 millilitres
1 qt.	app. 1.140 litres

Oven Temperatures

	°Fahrenheit	Gas Mark	°Celsius
Slow	300	2	140
	325	3	158
Moderate	350	4	177
	375	5	190
	400	6	204
Hot	425	7	214
	450	8	232
	500	9	260

Flour as specified in these recipes refers to Plain Flour unless otherwise described

Windmill Hill Thin Biscuits

2 oz. flour
½ oz. butter
½ teaspoon of baking powder
Pinch of salt
Milk

Set oven to 300°F or Mark 2. Sift together the flour, baking powder and salt and rub in the butter. Mix to a stiff paste with milk. Roll out thinly on a floured board, cut into circles, place on a greased baking sheet and bake until pale brown and crisp; approximately 10–15 minutes. If a 2 inch cutter is used to cut the pastry it should make 13 biscuits. Serve with a little butter and/or cheese.

Rabbit Stew

1 rabbit, jointed
Seasoned flour
1 oz. butter
½ pint good stock
½ pint ale or stout
½ teacup mushroom ketchup
Nutmeg
Lemon peel
1 onion stuck with 1 or 2 cloves

Set oven to 350 °F or Mark 4. Wash and dry the joints. Roll them in the flour and fry in the butter until brown. Add the stock, ale, ketchup, lemon peel and onion. Grate some nutmeg over all. Cook 1–2 hours, according to the age of the rabbit. Alternatively this could be simmered on top of the stove for a similar time.

Sussex Pudding

6 oz. suet
6 oz. raisins
6 oz. self-raising four
1 teaspoon mixed spice
2 eggs
¼ pint milk

Set oven to 375°F or Mark 5. Mix all the dry ingredients together. Mix the eggs with the milk and then combine with the dry ingredients. Pour into a greased tin approximately 8 inches long x 6½ inches wide and 2 inches deep. Bake for 1 hour. Serves 8.

Pevensey Castle

Apple Cracknell

FILLING
1lb. (approximately) sliced apples
Brown sugar to taste
1 oz. glacé or crystallised ginger, chopped

TOPPING
4 oz. self-raising flour 2½ oz. butter
2 oz. porridge oats
1 oz. brown sugar
1 teaspoon ground ginger

Set oven to 375°F or Mark 5. Fill a greased pie dish with thinly sliced apples and scatter the sugar and chopped ginger over them.

To make the topping, rub the fat into the flour and mix in the rest of the dry ingredients. Spread the mixture evenly over the apples. Bake till apples are soft and the top brown; approximately 25 minutes. Serves 4–5.

Ten-to-One Pie

8 oz. shortcrust pastry
8 oz. raw potato
2 medium onions
4 oz. left-over boiled bacon, ham or 'blanched' bacon rashers, chopped coarsley
Salt and pepper

Set oven to 400°F or Mark 6. Line a plate or 7 inch flan tin with half the pastry and fill with a layer of thinly sliced potato, a layer of sliced onion, a layer of meat, some seasoning and then more potatoes and onions. Cover with a pastry lid. Bake for 30 minutes, then reduce the temperature to 375°F or Mark 5 for a further 1 hour.

This can also be made with cooked potato and onions softened in butter or bacon fat and baked for approximately 30 minutes. Serves 5–6.

Chichester Cathedral from the Meadows